Macramé for Adult Beginners

Beginners

A Complete Guide To Macrame Basics,
Techniques, Knots And Advanced Projects

By

VIOLET MILES

Table of Content

Introduction

The complicated weaving method known as macramé originates in Africa and South America. Although tough, you only need a few simple knots to start. You will learn how to make many macramé crafts from this book. You can quickly prepare anything for yourself or your pals after you have mastered these basic procedures.

Today, the skill and pastime of macramé signify many different things to many individuals; in many ways, the skill is important and distinctive, yet it doesn't matter to others. Bonds are used in macramé to bind the hands and arms. Making a macramé item may be incredibly soothing and calming for the mind, body, and soul; it is also an option for ecologically responsible art. These are but a few of the advantages that admirers of macramé art think its practitioners get from this discipline.

In the book are wonderful crafts that are step-by-step outlined with a list of "you will need" materials. There are also a few micro project ideas so you can master a skill and start creating immediately. The project ideas demonstrate how the beauty of knots may be increased by selecting alternative threads or cords, thinner or thicker, based on how you want to utilize the design, while the method examples have been produced using standard cords for optimum clarity. You'll also learn how adding beads may improve the approaches and provide even more breathtaking effects.

Chapter 1: Macramé Basics

Macramé is often fastened to the work table using pins or a spring clip, contrasting knotted braids, typically done by hand. The square & a-half knot used with 3 or 4 cords is simple to master, after which you may move on to multi-strand methods and other half-hitch applications.

1. Macramé History

Macramé is said to have started with Arabic weavers who utilized knotting methods to make shawls, towels, and tapestries in the 13th century. It expanded to the remainder of the work and into Europe.

Throughout history, macramé has been popular in various eras, including the Victorian Era, the early 1970s, and the present. Macramé is still used to make fashionable wall hangings, belts, friendship bracelets, plant hangers, and purses.

2. How to Begin Using Macramé?

Macramé is simple to learn; you only need a little practice and some macramé cord. You will learn all you need to get started with this macramé book. This book demonstrates the materials you'll need, how to establish your workstation, and ways to tie all fundamental knots in macramé.

Macramé Supplies

To make macramé, you don't need difficult equipment or pricey materials.

You will often require the following:

- Rope

- Measuring tape

- Scissors

Cords made of various materials, such as cotton, hemp, linen, leather, jute, or wool, may be used to produce macramé. Special hardware, such as metal hoops, handbag handles, wooden rings, or belt buckles, are needed for certain designs. Other ornamental components, such as wood or glass beads, may be added.

Macramé's Best Rope

Cotton rope or twine makes the greatest kind of macramé cord. Cotton rope is readily accessible, soft, and flexible. It won't stretch out with time and is simple to knot. Cotton rope is reasonably priced and available online or at most craft shops. A 4 to 6mm 3-ply cotton cord is ideal for most home décor tasks. Select a cable diameter of less than 2mm for jewelry-making or micro-macramé applications.

Other Tools

You may use jute or hemp rope for a more natural, rustic appearance. Although working with these materials is a little more difficult, the ultimate result is textured and resilient. You may also use nylon paracord, leather cord, and rope made of polypropylene.

3. Is learning macramé simple?

Yes, learning macramé is simple. Although it initially seems difficult, macramé is a straightforward craft anybody can learn to accomplish.

When you master the fundamental macramé knots, you may combine them in various ways to make any design you can think of.

Estimating the lengths of cords

If you are switching the core and working cords, it might be difficult to determine the cable length for the working macramé, but as a general guideline, the core cords equal the length of the completed item plus 15cm (6inch) at either end for finishing.

For the working cables, allow 3 to 4 times the completed length.

4. How do we choose the best yarn?

In contrast to knitting yarn or crochet, macramé yarn is stiffer and often produced differently. Macramé yarn is braided or knotted together, unlike crochet and knitting yarns, which frequently consist of loose yarn strands. You may begin a macramé project using rope since it resembles rope more or, in some circumstances, really is rope. Your project's aesthetic is the major consideration when selecting the appropriate macramé yarn. Want to make a durable plant pendant with a knot? Then choose a thicker yarn, either cable or ropey. Are you planning to use the macramé method to create a bracelet? Then choose fine yarn. You can see how it is weaved together with this yarn. It provides a work with a somewhat more rugged appearance. This yarn is around 2mm thick and is in the middle range. With this yarn, you may start your first macramé creation and learn how to crochet.

5. Organizing your Workspace

You must set up a workstation for macramé before beginning a new project. Ensure you have enough space to move about comfortably and have appropriate illumination. You may work vertically on the hanging arrangement or horizontally over a flat table, depending on the nature and scope of your project.

Vertical Setup

A vertical workstation will be necessary for larger crafts, particularly wall hangings. Your work should be hung such that you can comfortably work on it.

The following are some ideas for hanging the piece:

- A wooden dowel rod may be hung from a clothes rack.

- On top of a door's back

- Using a doorknob

- Over a tall chair's back

A movable clothing rack is wise if you want to make many more wall hangings.

Horizontal Setup

You may do certain smaller crafts on a tabletop or other flat, horizontal surfaces. To keep the cords taut while you work, fasten the piece's beginning end to the table. You may fasten smaller items, such as macramé bracelets, beneath a clipboard's clip.

Chapter 2: Essential Tools and Equipment

Many of the tools and supplies mentioned are ones you will likely already have in your toolbox if you are an avid beader or crafter. Although you may always improvise, using a comparable material or the mentioned equipment and tools is advisable for optimal results. You don't need to buy everything at once.

1. Findings

Findings include all the tiny parts often made of metal and used to create and complete jewelry or various accessories.

Choosing the proper size and form of findings is crucial since they often conceal all raw ends of cords.

Maintain a wide variety of findings within your workbox so you may start and complete several works.

Cord ends

Single cables are finished with various types, some of which have lugs that can use pliers to tighten over the cord, while others are tubular, either attached with glue or a built-in crimp ring.

End cones

These bell or cone-shaped finds may be completed with a loop or a hole near the top.

Apply jewelry glue to fasten the braid through both styles for the greatest results.

Ribbon crimps

Although they may be utilized to complete flat braids or cable, as the name implies, they cover any raw end of the ribbon. Close your ribbon crimp around the braid using nylon-jaw pliers to protect it from harm.

Toggle fastening

This two-part fastening consists of a T-bar and a ring; to slide the T-bar into or out of the ring, turns it on its side. Choose a design element with additional ornamentation.

Trigger clasp

This low-cost clasp with a spring closing may finish necklaces and bracelets. The bolt ring and lobster claw are among the available designs.

Plastic clasps

These plastic clasps include a bar end that may be used to join cords, making them ideal for knotting methods like macramé. The clasps are offered in a variety of sizes and vibrant colors.

Finishing ends

Two ends of knotted ropes are finished with these findings. Every year, more and more types are produced, and the majority comes in various metallic finishes. Match your internal dimensions of finishing ends towards the cord or braid for optimal results. However, if this is not the case, certain finishing ends do not have a fastener.

Spring ends

These earlier types of finds might be formed like a cone or cylinder. Use pliers to tightly tighten one end ring to attach the braid or cord after tucking it within the wire coil.

End caps

Similar to end cones, end caps are round, square, or rectangular shapes that either feature a hole on the top or are pre-finished with a loop or ring. Apply jewelry glue to fasten the braid through both styles for the greatest results.

Jewelry fastenings

Findings of all kinds are used to complete jewelry items, including necklaces, bracelets, rings, and earrings. Please select a couple of fastening designs that work well with macramé.

Choose a style that fits the end cap and contrasts the braid in weight and color. Some fastenings, such as end caps, have magnetic fasteners built into their designs.

Magnetic fastenings

A powerful magnet has been included in the design of these tidy fasteners. They are ideal for completing bracelets and necklaces.

Multi-strand clasps

These come in a variety of designs. The slider closure is perfect for macramé and many other cuff-type bracelets, while the box form is appropriate for necklaces. According to the project, decide how many rings should be on each side.

2. Cords and Threads

Many different cords and threads may be used with macramé methods. The options are discussed in this section.

Choosing cords

Once you have mastered a technique, try it out on several materials; you may be surprised by the outcome. Knots may lose their definition when working with a delicate cord like embroidery cotton or satin rattail, but when using a firmer cord like wax cotton, Superlon™, or round leather thong, the form can be used be much clear. Choose your cable or thread following how you envision the end product will appear before you begin. Remember that these cords may be worked single or in many bundles and are offered in various thicknesses.

Cord guide

The representative board of cords offers a short overview of a few of the cords that are appropriate for macramé and a fast reference for the variety of thicknesses offered in the various cords.

Superlon™ 0.5mm
Superlon Tex™ (0.9mm) 400
cotton perle size 5
Chinese knotting cord 0.8mm
Chinese knotting cord 1.2mm
rattail 1.5mm
rattail 2mm
wax cotton 1mm
wax cotton 2mm
leather thong 1.5mm
leather thong 3mm
paracord 2mm
paracord 4mm

Chinese knotting cord

When worked, this nylon braided string maintains its spherical form. The finer cords, now available in 0.4-3mm, are often preferred for macramé. You can get the biggest color selections online. However, the bigger cables may not have as many color options as the finer cords.

Superlon™

Superlon™ often referred to as S-lon™, is a twisted nylon rope with industrial strength that was first used for upholstery. It is offered in widths of 0.5mm and 0.9mm, and both are appropriate for micro macramé plus other knotting methods where a delicate braid or finish is desired. These cords may be blended over thicker cords for a variety of textures and are ideal for adding beads to your knotting. Both sizes come in various neutral tones and attractive, modern hues.

Leather thong

Because it is a solid cord, a round leather thong forms a nice, identifiable knot. It is offered in various thicknesses, ranging from around 0.5mm to 6mm. The larger cords are better to be used, creating a core to tie knots around, while the smaller cords work well for tying knots. There are many different colors and natural tones of leather thongs. The varying thicknesses of snakeskin impression cords and pearlescent finishes, often in soft pastel colors, are extremely beautiful.

Embroidery threads

Only two easily accessible threads suitable for macramé are stranded cotton and cotton perlé. Although embroidery threads are delicate and won't maintain a knot's form securely, they look beautiful when paired with stronger cords.

Since the color selection is significantly wider than other cables, interesting color combinations are available. Metallic embroidery threads may hint at glitter even though embroidery threads are typically matte.

Satin cord (rattail)

This high-shine, silky rope comes in a variety of thicknesses: rattail has 2mm thick, mouse-tail is 1.5mm thick, and bug tail is 1mm thick; nevertheless, these days, all three are often referred to as rattail. Due to the cord's relative softness, knot shapes are not supported effectively, and it is not a particularly durable material.

Wax cotton cord

A variety of methods work well with wax cotton cords. Keep an eye out for the 3mm cord, which is thicker and works especially well for single and braided knots since it keeps its form well. For macramé, thinner wax cotton works best since it's simple to thread beads on. They come in various colors, some in keeping with current fashion trends and natural tones. Pull it under a medium-hot iron to correct kinks and restore the finish when the wax cotton cord weakens from repeated usage or if you wish to reuse a length.

Paracord

This thick cable's two most typical thicknesses are paracord 450 (2mm) and paracord 550 (4mm), which have four central strands each. Because it is rather hefty, paracord is well-suited for producing bracelets plus other accessories using single knots. It is also popular for men's jewelry. The cable comes in various solid, dark, and bright hues and multicolored patterns.

Faux suede

The flat microfiber cord has a suede-like appearance similar to genuine leather, but it is considerably more malleable and gives knots an entirely different appearance. It often comes in a variety of colors and is 3mm broad.

3. Beads

All macramé methods may have beads added in some way, either during the knotting process or subsequently.

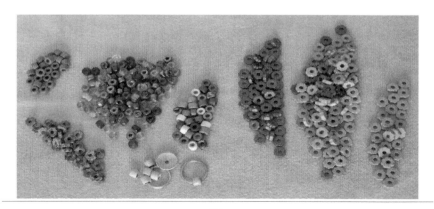

Choosing beads

Although beads come in a wide variety of colors, sizes, finishes, and forms, the size of the hole is crucial when knotting so that the beads can be strung onto the rope effortlessly. If you're going bead shopping, it is a smart option to have a piece of cord with you.

Large beads

You may choose from a wide variety of beads, from basic wood beads to magnificent pearls and crystals, to use with knotting methods.

The size of the bead hole need not be a limitation since certain beads, like those in the Swarovski Mini bead line, have remarkably big holes that allow even the 6mm beads to fit onto a 1mm chain. Large holes in Pandora-style beads let them slide over 6mm wire.

Seed beads

It is a collective word for the small glass beads utilized mostly for stringing and sewing. Rocailles, or basic seed beads, cylinder-shaped beads, also called magnificas or delicas, have bigger holes and can be strung into 1mm rope. The most popular sizes are 15 to 3 (1-5.5mm), with 15 (1mm) representing the smallest. Watch out for uncommon forms and textures, like papillon (even peanut) beads & magatamas, as well as textures like triangular, hex, or Charlotte beads (drop beads).

Focal beads

These huge beads are often utilized as the center of attention for jewelry designs. Using a bail, you can hang pendant beads and create macramé. You can connect cords to big beads rings. Also, remember that you may string huge beads between two pieces of macramé with end caps.

Chapter 3: Techniques and Knots

1. Gathering Knot

The collecting knot often called a wrapping knot, is a closing knot used to join ropes. These are also at the tip of the macramé plant hangers.

Two threads in this knot are functional; the other strings will serve as filler cords.

It would be best if you constructed a long, downward-facing loop (u-shaped) over your filler cord ring using a separate cable length that will serve as your working cord.

1. Wrap the functional cable around filler cords and string, starting below the top-end, which points upwards.

2. Make sure the loop is left exposed for some time.

3. Insert the end of the wrapping thread into the loop at the base of your wrappings.

4. Grab the end of the cable sticking upward to place the rope under the wraps.

5. Draw first before the coil is encased through the wraps. The knot insert has been finished.

6. You may cut the working cable at both ends if you want a smooth finish.

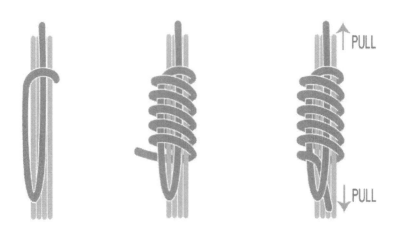

The hump is hidden at the rear of your knot since your reverse lark head knot is tied in the other direction.

1. Place that loop you just created beneath the dowel pin after cutting the rope in half. Drag those two cords that stretch around the thread while dragging the coil across the front side.

2. Any project would benefit from starting with this knot, which may also serve as the project's basis. Wherever you obtain your macramé materials, use a thin cable for this. You may get one online or at craft shops.

3. You shouldn't hurry, and make sure the tension is consistent throughout. You will discover that creating is not at all difficult once you practice.

4. Use both hands to ensure everything is level and well-secured as you work. You may use tweezers to make it tight over the string's base.

5. To tie the knot, equally draw each thread down towards the base string with both hands.

6. Once again, maintain evenness at the base while you tug the center to tighten the knot against the guide rope.

7. Make sure that all your knots are tight and solid throughout the completed item, and do your best to ensure they are all equal. It will take practice before you can do it properly every time, but keep in mind that practice makes perfect, so with enough time, and you should accomplish it without too many difficulties.

8. Make sure everything is balanced, safe, and tied off. You are prepared to depart after you tie up any loose ends.

2. Lark's Head Knot

It may serve as the project's basis and is a limitless foundation knot for every endeavor. Use a thin cord; you can get it from craft shops, online, or wherever you get the macramé materials.

Spend some time ensuring you are working with the right string and at the right stage of the project.

Work the cord around the string's end using a base string as the knot's central component. As you wrap your string around the cord's base, check to ensure everything is even.

Once you pull the cord through the piece's center, tie a slip knot across the string's base, keeping the ends even.

When the project is finished, check that all your knots are even and secure. It will take practice before you can do it perfectly every time, but keep in mind that practice makes perfect, so with enough time, you will be able to do it without too much difficulty.

Make sure everything is level, safe, and tied off. You're all set to go after you tie up any loose ends.

3. Overhand Knot

A straightforward knot called the overhand knot is used to connect many ropes. It's possible to utilize many cords or even just one.

1. Circulate the thread in a circle.

2. Your strings' ends should be closed around the coil by moving them.

4. Reverse Lark's Head Knot

It is a wonderful first knot that may serve as the project's basis. For this, use a thin cord; you can acquire this, too, in craft shops or online, in addition to the macramé materials.

Do not hurry, and make sure the tension is consistent throughout. You will discover that creating is not difficult if you use the examples as guides. Use both hands to ensure that everything is equal and snug as you work. You may use tweezers to pull it tight against the string's base.

To tie the knot, equally draw each thread down against the base string with both hands.

Keep the base level while pulling the center to tighten the knot against the guiding rope.

Make sure all your knots are tight and secure throughout the process and check to see that they are equal. Before you can do it correctly every time, you will need to practice. However, keep in mind that practice makes perfect, so with enough time, you should be able to accomplish it without excessive difficulty.

5. Clove Hitch

The clove hitch often called a double half hitch, creates a row in your work. Sometimes, we may work vertically, horizontally, or diagonally.

A sequence of knots will connect your macramé creation called a horizontal clove hitch. Your filler rope forms the first chord within the knot, and the other cords are working cables.

1. Lay the filler cable horizontally across the remaining strands of the left chord.

2. Please take the next cable, the first working cord, and move it forward, up, and over the filler cord to the left to form a counterclockwise circle.

3. Take the same rope and move it up through and across the circle to the right of your initial knot. Now, two ties will be placed side by side. The hook tie parallel to the clove is what it is.

4. Utilizing your subsequent operational rope and the same filler string, untangle the clove hook's knots.

5. Before you get the desired knot or design, keep building the ties.

The diagonal clove hitch creates a series of diagonal links for your project.

1. Place one filler chord diagonally across the remaining strings using the chord on the left.

2. Follow the horizontal clove hitches' measures two through four, going diagonally instead of straight through.

3. Repeat until you get the ideal feeling.

6. Capuchin Knot

Any project may be started with this knot, which serves as the project's base. Make use of a thin cable for this.

Spend some time making sure you are utilizing the appropriate string at the appropriate stage of the project.

As you go with the craft, start from the base rope and tie the knot onto it.

Twist the cord twice, and then draw the thread through the middle to create the knot.

Make sure everything is level, safe, and tied off. You're all set to go after you tie up any loose ends.

7. Spiral Stitch

A sequence of half knots is used to construct a spiral stitch, sometimes referred to as either the half-knot spiral or a half-knot sinnet. It is an ornamental stitch that is very significant to your team. A minimum of four strings, two functional strings, plus two filler cords are needed for the spiral stitch. However, it may have more. These strings change from left to right and have internal labels of 1 to 4. The active strings are strings one and four, whereas strings two and three are filler strings. These instructions show how to make the spiral stitch on its left side. However, you could start on the right and make the proper side using half knots.

1. Take work cord 1 and place it beneath operating cord 4 and to the right of your filler cables.

2. Working cord one should be moved over working cord four while moving to the west and beneath the filler's cables.

3. Stretch the cables around the filling after removing all of the working wires.

4. Maintain the previous direction while permitting further half-ties.

5. As you work, the cables will keep swirling.

8. Crown Knot

This wonderful first knot may serve as the project's basis. Make use of a thin cable for this.

Never haste, and make sure there is constant tension. You will discover that creating is not difficult if you use the examples as guides.

As you work, use a pin to assist holds everything in place.

Thread the threads together in a web like pattern. To assist you in understanding what is happening, it is helpful to practice with various colors.

Repeat for the subsequent row on the outside, pulling the knot firmly this time. To make the knot, repeat this as frequently as you desire. Following the project, you may create it as thick as you'd like. On the same cable, you may add additional lengths.

Please make sure all of your knots are tight and solid throughout the final plan, and do your hardest to ensure they are all equal. Make sure everything is level, safe, and tied off. You're all set to go after you tie up any loose ends.

9. Half Knots and Square Knots

The square knot, which may be formed with either a left- or right-facing orientation, is among the most popular macramé knots. The half-knot is rectangle-shaped. Depending on the side you work from, this might be facing left or right.

Square knots need a minimum of four cords, including two active cords plus two filler strings. However, they sometimes need more. The opening and closing strings are known as the Operating Strings. They will be referred to as cord 1 with cord 4 running. We'll mention cables two and three as they are filler cables in the center. Such cords change places but keep their original numbering.

The finished knot features a vertical hump on the left side of a square knot facing the left.

1. Take your first cable, operational cord 1, cross it over the middle cords, filler cords 2 and 3, move it to the right, and then pass it underneath your last cord, operative cord 4.

2. Move operational cord four to the west, over operational cord one, and beneath all filler cords.

3. All of the operational cables should be pushed in parallel to the filler. It has a westward-facing half-square knot shape. Currently, operational chord number four is on the left, and functional cord number one is on the right.

4. Take running cable 1, cross it under operating cord 4, and then pass it through the 2 filler cords towards the left.

5. Move cord four, which is in good working order, to the right, beneath all the filler strings and overworked cord 1. All threads that are in motion should be pulled and tied.

6. Hold the wires erect on the fabric. It completes the left-side square knot.

The finished knot has a vertical hump, as does the half-knot, with a square knot facing its right side.

1. The last chord (cord 4) should be moved to the west, passing beneath an initial cord (cord 1) and crossing the filler cords (strings 2 and 3).

2. Working cord 1 should be pushed to the center, above working cable 4, and under the filler cords.

3. Make it apparent by pulling and locking all strings. That is a right-facing half-square knot.

4. Working cord 1 is now on the right, while working cord four is on the left since the placements of the functional cables have been switched.

5. Work cord four to the outside, over the filler cables, and below cord 1.

6. Move job chord 1 above working cord 4 and below the filler cables to the west.

7. All threads that are in motion should be pulled and tied. It looks like a knot in a right-facing square.

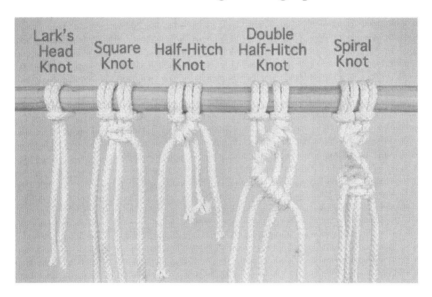

10. Diagonal Double Half-Knot

For ornaments, basket hangings, or any other tasks requiring you to lay weight on the object, utilize this seamless knot.

Use a heavier-weight cord you can get online or at craft supply shops.

Do not hurry, and make sure the strain is constant. You'll discover that creating is not at all difficult since practice makes perfect.

Start twisting from the top of the project and work your way down. As you go through the piece, keep it equal. As you move down the length, tie your knots in 4-inch intervals.

Watch the picture to see where to put the knots as you weave in and out. Again, practicing with various colors will help you realize what you must accomplish at each stage of the piece.

Make sure that all your knots are tight and solid throughout the completed project, and do your best to ensure they are all equal. Keep in mind that practice makes perfect. Make sure everything is level, safe, and tied off. Close off all the gaps.

11.   Square Knot

Any project would benefit from starting with this knot, which may also serve as the project's basis. Wherever you obtain your macramé materials, use a thin cable for this. You may get one online or at craft shops. Take your time, and make sure the tension is consistent throughout. It is not at all difficult to design, and practice makes perfect.

Once you're done, check to see that all of your knots are strong and secure overall, and do your utmost to ensure they are all equal. It will take practice before you can do it properly every time, but keep in mind that practice makes perfect, so with enough time, and you should be able to do it without too much difficulty.

Make sure everything is balanced, safe, and tied off. You are prepared to depart after you tie up any loose ends.

12. Frivolité Knot

It might serve as the project's fundamental framework. For this as well, use a thin cable. It may be purchased online or at craft shops. There's no need to hurry, and ensure the tension is consistent throughout. You may realize that creating is rather simple. Make a knot onto this while using your base string as a guide to keeping it in place. This knot is fairly simple to tie.

Pull the cord's end up and into the middle.

When finished, check that your knots are equal, secure, and strong. Make sure everything is level, safe, and tied off. Close off all the gaps.

13. Chinese Crown Knot

It might serve as the project's fundamental framework. Wherever you obtain your macramé materials, use a thin cable for this. You may get one online or at craft shops. Take your time, and make sure the tension is consistent throughout. You'll discover that creating is not at all difficult since practice makes perfect.

As you work, use a pin to assist everything in place. As shown in the photographs, weave the threads together, interspersing. To help you notice what's happening, experiment using several colors. Continue for the row outside after tightening the knot.

To form the knot, repeat this as frequently as you desire. Following the project, you may create it as thick as you'd like. On the same cable, you may add additional lengths.

Please ensure all of your knots are tight and solid throughout the completed job, and do your hardest to ensure they are all equal. It will take practice before you can do it properly every time, but keep in mind that practice makes perfect, so with enough time, you should be able to accomplish it without much difficulty.

Make sure everything is balanced, safe, and tied off. You are prepared to depart after you tie up any loose ends.

14.   Josephine Knot

Use this knot for ornaments, basket lynching's, or any other tasks where you'll need to add weight to the object. Use a heavier-weight cord you can get online or at craft supply shops.

To move the cables properly, take your time. Do not hurry, and check that the cables are evenly tensioned through.

Work on bigger sections at once while using the pins and the knots you are making. As you work on the project throughout the piece, this will assist you in maintaining it.

To create the ring in the middle of the strings, pass the ends of knots through the loops. When you're finished, check your knots to make sure they're tight and secure and that they're all distributed evenly. Before you can do anything correctly, you'll need to practice. Make sure everything is level, safe, and tied off. Close off all the gaps.

15.   Horizontal Double Half-Knot

It might serve as the project's base foundation. Purchase a thin cable for this from your preferred source for macramé materials.

To ensure that you use the right string at every project step, follow the instructions carefully and take your time. Make sure the tension is consistent throughout. You'll discover that creating is not at all difficult since practice makes perfect.

Start twisting from the top of the project and work your way down. As you go through the piece, keep it equal. Making the way down the whole thing, tie your knots with 4-inch intervals.

Once you're done, check that every knot is firm and tight throughout, and try your hardest to ensure they are all even.

As soon as everything is even and fastened, knot off loose ends.

16. RYA Knot

Anyone can appreciate a fine tassel. A rya knot would be a quick and simple method to give your weaving or macramé patterns excitement and movement.

Cut a 25-centimeter string into about 6 pieces. Depending on how thick and lengthy you want the tassels to be, the length and quantity of cord may vary.

Tie a semi-square knot.

Fold the six pieces of cord in half to create a loop, ensuring the ends of each piece of cord touch. Put the center of that loop on top of the filler cables 2 and 3.

When bringing the ends of cords one and four to the front, pass all sides of the cables through the space between cords 1-2 and 3-4. Pull a little bit on these cables.

Till the tassel has been produced, firmly pull both cords 1 and 4. Finish the half-square knot you started in step 2 by forming a second half-square knot if you want to secure it more firmly.

You may now brush the bottoms of the tassels if you used a cotton rope with one ply. You may do this by beginning at the ends and working your way up with a hair comb. For a finish that looks more polished, you may alternatively utilize a wooden slicker brush.

Cut off any extra length to get the tassels to the length you want.

Chapter 4: Beginner Projects

Little motivational projects are scattered throughout this chapter that may be completed as a simple and fast extension to the different methods and doesn't need any more training. Detailed step-by-step directions are provided for you to follow, and some gorgeous patterns below highlight your favorite methods. As needed, you should go back to the braiding and knotting methods.

1. Knot Double coin cuff

Double coin knots are often made one after the other in the same manner; however, if the knot is started on the left, next to the right, and so forth, the knot will lay flattered.

Long strands loop over these double coin knots that alternate at the top and bottom margins of the cuff to produce a beautiful design.

Materials

- Magnetic fastening having 3x9mm internal dimension end caps

- 2mm Leather cord, 10 yards or 9mm

Directions

1. Make three equal, 3 m (3 1/3 yard) long strands of the leather cord. Regarding Chinese knots: Double Coin Knot, beginning with a clockwise loop in the left hand

and dragging your working end (right-hand tail) back over the loop to form a double coin knot with all three strands. Complete and tighten the knot so your top loop is sizable and the three strands remain flat and properly spaced.

2. Create a secondary double coin knot by beginning with a loop in the right hand, bringing your working end (left tail) down throughout the loop, wrapping the other tail around it, and then doubling back to form the knot.

3. Firmen the second knot, modifying its placement, so it is somewhat near the first knot without touching it. Verify that almost all the cords remain flat inside the knot and are not twisted in any way.

4. Using the tail that emerges from the previous knot, you immediately recognize which side to construct the loop on.

5. Double coin knots should be tied after each other, with the start position changing every time.

6. After tying six knots, measure the length of a cuff. If necessary, alter the space between each knot to account for the fastening.

7. After the last knot, cross the cords over one another. Wrap the cables together or stitch them across to keep them flat, depending on the design of the end cap. Cut

off the ends and use epoxy resin glue to attach them to the end caps.

2. Switchback Bracelet

There is no fixed design for this bracelet; you may create it using your custom arrangement of various knotting methods. Check the placement of the bracelet's beads as you go since they must be on top of the wrist instead of below. Work the bracelet for around 51 cm (20 inches) until it wraps around the wrist three times.

Materials

- 3 ¼ yards or 3m each of 1mm & 1.5mm wax cotton cord, brown

- Swarovski Elements: Square Mini-beads, eight 6mm light silk

- Metal button

- Map pins and Pinboard (optional)

- 1 ½ yard or 1.25m of 1mm pearlized leather cord, Off-white

- 5 ½ yard or 5m Superlon™, cream Tex 400 (0.9mm)

- 8 size Double Delicas seed beads, approx. 50 topaz dark rainbow 103

- Epoxy resin adhesive or E6000 jewelry glue

Directions

1. The leather cord is folded in half. Use a lark's head knot to wrap a brief waste cord around the pearlized leather to avoid damage, then fasten it to a work table or pinboard.

2. Using the Switchback Braids and a 1.5mm wax cotton cord: Work an 8 cm (3 in) length of normal switchback braid across the leather cord using the single cord switchback braid technique. Adjust the loop's size after approximately 2.5 cm (1 in) to fit the bracelet's button, and then continue.

3. Select 14 double delicas and place one on the leather cord's other end. Drop one of the wax cotton cord's tails, then use a stitched switchback technique to slide beads up through the knots and secure them as you make the subsequent knot.

4. Work an 8 cm (3 in) length of standard switchback after switching to the cream Superlon™ Tex. Work your initial half of a square knot in macramé. The second tail of the cord should be fed through the opening in the opposite direction after you pick up the square mini-bead with one string.

5. To make it simpler to pass the cable through the bead, melt the cord's end with a lighter and cut it.

6. To ensure that the bead sits flat, wrap both leather cords in a square knot. Seven additional mini-beads should be added, each time tying a square knot. Add another 2.5 cm (1 in) of the cream switchback.

7. Work on the second half of your bracelet as you normally would, varying the cord thickness, switching from stitched switchback to ordinary switchback, adding double Delicas beads, or working one length without beads if you see fit. Add a length of standard switchback constructed with a 1mm wax cord to complete.

8. Check the length, and fasten the button to the leather cords' ends. Trim the leather, then use epoxy resin or the E6000 jewelry adhesive to attach it to the button's backside.

3. Knotted Prosperity Belt

A prosperity knot is a huge, flat, rectangle-shaped knot ideal for forming a belt. Simply tying prosperity knots just after the other will work, but incorporating a dual coin knot somewhere between will keep the belt flatter and enable more precise length adjustment with the buckle. You might adorn it by putting beads in the spaces among the knots or by hanging charms from 1 or 2 of the loops.

Materials

- Half-inch or 12mm wide buckle

- E6000 jewelry glue

- 9 yard or 8.5m of 2mm wax cotton cord

- Small leather piece

Directions

1. Beginning with one loop in your left hand, fold your cord into half to locate the center, then tie a dual coin knot there. Continue tying a loose prosperity knot following Chinese Knots: Prosperity Knot. To firm up, move each overlapping cord toward the knot's top one at a time, stopping until only two loops remain.

2. Pull your top left cable through to raise its bottom loop on 1 side. Repeat on the other side. To strengthen the knot, draw each tail one at a time.

3. Repeat this firming-up procedure to get a tightly woven prosperity knot 12mm (12 inches) wide. Holding your knot firmly between the thumbs and fingers of two hands, move the strands a little to make a uniform weave.

4. Starting this time with a loop in your right hand, tie the double coin knot using the tails. Once the knot is made, move it near the prosperity knot without touching it. Because you won't be able to change it afterward, firm it up carefully.

5. Continue making double coins and alternating prosperity knots. Change the side on which the initial loop is placed for the prosperity knot and the double coin knot.

6. Put an end to the belt after tying the prosperity knot after it reaches the proper length, allowing for overlap. To close the gap, wrap the ends twice around the belt buckle on each side. Then, stitch the opposite side shut.

7. Cut a leather strip that measures 1 x 3 cm (1/8 x 1 1/8 in) to create the belt loop. Stick the leather strip over stitched cord ends underneath the buckle by applying adhesive to one end of the leather strip.

8. Leave a loop big enough for the second end of a belt to pass through after wrapping the strip around the belt to ensure it crosses the back.

9. As soon as the glue is applied to the overlapping strip, please keep it in place until it dries. Wait 24 hours before using.

4. Rhinestone Bracelets

Making delicate jewelry with micro macramé is easy by using a thin knotting rope.

The outside cords may be embellished with seed beads to create a straightforward beaded bracelet, or for a touch of glitz, they can be knotted over a rhinestone cup chain.

Materials

- 2 yard or 2.5m of 1mm knotting cord, nylon

- Pinboard and map pins (optional)

- 4-inch or 11cm of 4mm rhinestone cup chain, stretched-out

- E6000 jewelry glue

Directions

1. Cut the knotting rope to 50 cm (20 in), and then fold both strands in half. The short length containing the loop at the top should be pinned or taped to the work surface. Make an overhand knot with the larger piece of cord and wrap it around the shorter piece.

2. Work 3 cm (1 in) in square knots for a bracelet that measures 17.5 cm (7 in). To keep the knots in place, attach a pin or piece of tape to the bottom.

3. Place the cup chain's length atop those two cord threads. Every rhinestone on your cup chain should have one square knot between them. Start your next square knot using the right cord if the bar is on the right side of the last square knot; if it is located on its left, start using the left cord. To balance the square knots, continue tying square knots between each rhinestone and switch which side you start the knot on.

4. Square knots in a 3 cm (1 in) piece or working the length to fit the other end will finish the macramé. Verify the bracelet's length and make any required adjustments. Over two cords, tie a 2-strand button knot by weaving your cords in pairs. When the button knot is approximately 3-5mm (in-out) from the square knots, gently tighten it by pushing the cords through.

5. When the glue has cured, clip the cords that emerge at the base of a button knot where you've applied a little adhesive. Verify that the bracelet's opposite end loop fits snuggly over the button knot. You may make a little adjustment by pushing the macramé knots up or down on the center core cords.

6. Dab some adhesive on the backside to keep the loop in place and at the proper size. To achieve a cleaner transition to the macramé, flip your overhand knot to the other side once you've knotted it.

5. Beaded necklace

To make this lovely macramé necklace stand out, look for a large focal bead. With the attractive mottled texture and sophisticated style, the beads give a conventional method a very contemporary look. Fine wax cotton or string is perfect in place of a paper jewelry cord if you cannot get it.

Materials

- Rectangular gold and brown accent bead, 4 x 2.5cm large
- 24 heishi beads, gold-plated
- Toggle fastening, gold-plated
- Scissors
- 3m each of 1mm paper jewelry cord in cream, brown and beige
- Gold and brown round beads, two 15mm plus four 12mm
- 2 Leather crimps, gold-plated
- Low tack tape
- Flat-nosed pliers

Directions

1. Place the huge rectangular bead in the center of the three cables after feeding it onto them. Ensure the cords are vertical before taping the bead toward the work surface. Then, tape the cables above the bead.

2. With the beige and dark brown cords, tie three half knots around the cream core thread. Add a heishi bead, and then tie three more half knots. Work another series of three half knots with a second heishi bead. Permit the knots to twist naturally.

3. Grab a sizable spherical bead from each of the three strands. Recurring Step 2 Repeat step 2 using a little round bead available. Pick up the second little circular bead.

4. After the last little round bead, repeat step 2 six more times to add the heishi beads. Work a basic half knot for around 8 cm (3 inches), allowing the cords to twist freely.

5. Turn the center bead around because the second pair of cords is pointing in your direction after removing the tape from it. To finish the second side of the necklace, repeat step 2 once more. Try your necklace on to see how it fits, then add half knots as necessary. Although a longer necklace might be created, the completed length must be about 48 cm (19 inches).

6. Cut the rope ends to a 6mm (1/4 inch) length. Leather crimp ends are used to secure the ends. Use gold-plated jump rings to join each end to a toggle fastener. Select several smaller beads having holes big enough to accommodate 4 parts of thread together with a large focal bead.

6. Braid Round Earrings

These classy earrings are simple to build and are embellished with Swarovski Elements, featuring lovely Baroque pendants. A fine, strong braid is created with Superlon™, a stiff nylon cable, and the earrings are completed with premium end caps made specifically for two 4-5mm strands.

Materials

- Sewing needle and thread

- XILION beads 5328, two 6mm pacific opal, two 6mm ruby

- Two Silver silk Capture end cap gunmetal having 8 x 9mm internal dimensions, double-strand

- Two gunmetal jump rings

- Two gunmetal earring wires

- Weight approx. 4 oz. or 100g

- Jewelry tools

- 39-inch or 1m each of Superlon™ cord in deep pink, steel grey, dark grey, and teal

- 2 Baroque pendant 6090, 16mm ruby

- 2 Crystal pearl 5810, 6mm Tahitian-look

- Two gunmetal headpins

- Two gunmetal triangle bails

- Kumihimo disk

- Sewing thread

- Nylon-jaw pliers

Directions

1. To prepare the Superlon™ threads, carefully press with a medium steam iron to remove any kinks and soften the thread. The cables should be arranged in the beginning position after folding the cord bundle in half and setting up the disc.

2. Concerning round braids: Work a length of 20 cm (8 in) for Round Braid 2.

3. Take your braid from the disc, and then wrap it with sewing thread close to the end. Wrap one more, and then measure 8 cm (3 in). After leaving a tiny space, wrap the thread again and measure another 8 cm (3 in) in length. Close to the wrapping, split the braid in half.

4. One of the circular braid sections should be used, and the ends should be inserted in one of its end caps before being tightened using nylon-jaw pliers. To create the second earring, repeat.

5. Every Baroque pendant bead should have a triangular bail attached to it before a jump ring. Put a jump ring between the braid's ends and discretely fasten it with a few small stitches.

6. Grab a ruby XILION bead and one pacific opal XILION bead upon a headpin to create the bead dangles. Create a substantial loop, and then attach it to one of your short braid lengths. For the second earring, repeat.

7. Open the loop on one earring wire and connect it to the loop on its end cap to complete each earring.

7. Macramé brooch

When done with fine cords, macramé, often considered a very simple chunky knotting method, becomes an exquisite micro macramé. Use complementary hues to get a rainbow effect across a lovely brooch.

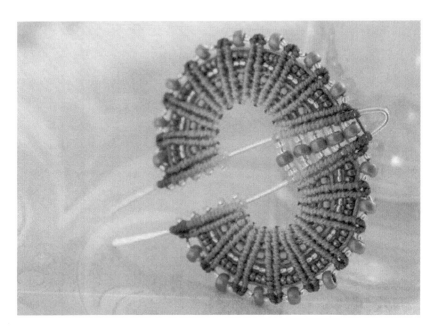

Materials

- 8-inch or 20cm of 1mm or 19swg half-hard sterling silver wire

- Gold Raspberry luster

- Brooch back

- Needle and thread

- Map pins

- Spring clip (optional)

- 1 ¾ yard or 1.5m each of Superlon™ cord in purple, coral, lilac, light grey, plus dusky pink

- Seed beads: size 6 (3.5mm) matte silver, size 11 (2.2mm) silver-lined crystal and emerald, size 10 (2mm) color-lined peach

- 10 cm Ultrasuede™ 4 inch square

- Jewelry tools

- Foam core board

- Adhesive tape

Directions

1. Bend your silver wire in half to form a 'V' shape with a slightly rounded end. Superlon™ cords should be arranged in the following sequence before use: lilac, purple, light grey, coral, and dusky pink.

2. Please pick up a purple string seed bead with a silver-lined crystal and place it in the middle. With 1 side of the "V," place the rope folded in half over the wire. To tie a reverse lark's head knot, pass the tails through the loop and over the wire.

3. Work each side's half-hitch. With the remaining colored cords, continue steps 2 and 3, each time adding a bead.

4. Tape the wire form into place after placing it onto the foam core board. Bring the purple cord's end over the wire to be parallel. Put each cord through a double half-hitch one at a time.

5. Place a map pin in the rib's end, and then slightly slant a purple cord across vertical cords. Use a spring clip or tape to secure. The first grey cord and the dusky pink cords make twin half-hitches. Work double half-hitches again after picking up a peach seed bead with a colored line on the subsequent grey cord.

6. Double half-hitches should be worked with the initial coral cord before picking up 2 silver-lined crystal seed beads and securing them with another double half-hitch. On the first lilac cord, thread 3 emerald raspberry gold luster seed beads and secure with double half-hitches.

7. Finish using a silver-lined crystal, the size 6 matte silver, and the silver-lined crystal on the last purple string after doing double half-hitches on the subsequent lilac cord. Practice the final double half-hitch.

8. Based on your tension, repeat with * six to seven times until the macramé semicircle turns to meet the wire once again. Work a straight half-hitch rib with the purple cord while returning to the edge's outer position. Work double half-hitches over the wire with each chord in turn.

9. All cord tails should be tucked beneath the silver wire. Please choose one size 6 matte silver seed bead and two silver-lined crystals, and place them on the first dusky

pink cord. On the opposite side of the wire 'V,' work a double half-hitch. Next, fasten the bead-free dusky pink cord.

10. Repeat on these two grey cords, and then work your way down the wire, putting beads of each color on the first row. As the distance between the wires becomes smaller, you may use fewer silver-lined beads.

11. Working in macramé, create a semicircle that matches the first side and finishes with a smooth half-hitch rib. With the first cord, make a double half-hitch and add a crystal with a silver lining. To secure the bead, do a double half-hitch using the same rope. Repeat for every additional cord.

12. The cord should be folded over the back of a macramé, and invisible stitches should be made. Cut cleanly. Each semicircle of Ultrasuede™ is cut to fit it, and the edges are then covertly stitched in place.

13. To conceal the small stitch between the macramé knots, sew a brooch back to 1 side on the back of the brooch by going across to the right side and then returning through to the reverse. Securely sew the ends together.

14. The angle of a half-hitch rib will be determined by the beads added to the vertical cords.

8. Beads Plant Hanger

Making a plant hanger is a lot of fun. It uses the spiral knot, which is fulfilling and looks like a DNA strand, and gives you the option to construct your custom beads if you choose. If you want to use air-dry clay to produce the beads, you must manufacture them a minimum of 24 hours ahead of time to allow for thorough drying. Pick up a piece of air-dry clay, spin it in your hands to form a spherical, and if you desire to be more artistic and have fun experimenting, cut some embellishments into it using a little toothpick. Remember to pierce a hole in the center with a pen or pencil!

Materials

- 5 cm wooden ring

- Large eye knitting needle

- Scissors

- 21.6 m cotton braided rope with having 5 mm diameter

- Terracotta air-dry clay or any 3 beads of your choice shop-bought having a 4 mm hole

- Tape measure

- Hook

Directions

Note: In general, employ consistent pressure while tying each knot using the braided rope. Since this rope has a little more flexibility than a 1 - 3 ply reused cotton rope, it is preferable to tie a looser knot.

1. The wooden ring should first be hung on a hook. Six braided cord segments are threaded through a wooden ring.

2. The simplest method to achieve this is to thread the six pieces of rope through the ring collectively rather than one at a time. The cable lengths on each side of the ring should be about equal.

3. Make one gathering knot of about 4 cm in length with 1 of the thinner cotton strands.

4. The 12 cords should be divided into three groups of 4. Tie 30 spiral knots with the first set of 4 cords. With the remaining 2 groups, repeat this.

5. Take the cords closest to the outside and thread them around the bead after passing them between the inner cords.

6. Knot 30 spirals in a row.

7. On either 2 groups, repeat steps 4 and 5.

8. Take the two right-hand cords of every group and the two left-hand cords of a group towards your right of this one, leaving an 18 cm space. Make a square knot using

these 4 cords. Repeat this procedure twice, working to your right, to connect all the cables.

9. Repeat step 6 while keeping a 6 cm space.

10. Tie a gathering knot about 4 cm long with the little additional cord. Once you've cut the plant hanger's tail to the desired length, you're done!

9. Heart Keychain

Materials

- 1 bead, big

- 8 beads, small (optional)

- 8 threads, 2.7 inches long each

Directions

1. A knot will be tied overhand. Make a loop over the top of folded thread after taking one thread and folding it in

half. You may measure the loop length using the thumb as a reference. Holding the thread during this length will isolate the loop.

2. Make a second loop with the remaining thread while keeping the original loop separate. While holding onto the original loop, thread the original loop around the new loop. When done, pull to tighten.

3. Place a different thread over the knotted portion of the previous thread, making sure the knot is located in the center of the new thread you just used.

4. You will now make a square knot. Take the unknotted left-hand side of a thread you just laid down, cross it across the thread above it, and tuck the right-hand thread beneath it. The right side thread should then be threaded around the loop that the left side thread has made, under your thread at the bottom, and on the left side. Pull all threads on the right and left sides in unison so that they tighten and form a knot.

5. Place the lone thread on your right beneath the left thread and underneath the 2 threads in the center. Take your left thread now and pass it through the loop on the right and beneath the 2 threads in the center. Your knot will be formed by pulling to simultaneously tighten both sides.

6. The single thread on the left should be taken, followed by its single thread on the right. Make sure the threads are both horizontal. To put the left side aside until later, you will only be dealing with the right side for the time being.

7. Fold a single fresh thread in half, carefully leaving a loop at the top. After that, tuck the thread beneath the rightmost single thread and fold the top over. Pull these two loose threads into the loop's center to resemble the image above. The Lark's Head knot will then result by pulling the threads such that they tighten.

8. Repeat step 7 with two additional single threads to create two additional Lark's head knots upon that right side.

9. Take your left single thread, which, as was previously explained, should be horizontal. On your left single thread, tie three additional Lark's head knots.

10. Now, each side of you must have three lark head knots.

11. Now the center should have two threads. Please pick up a little bead, and then thread the two threads with it.

12. Take a large bead and press it onto the same thread.

13. To secure the beads, tie a straightforward overhand knot at the end of the main thread below the beads.

14. Use scissors to remove the extra thread at the knot's end, leaving the knot alone.

15. Take the first thread on the right from the left group of the threads and lay it horizontally over the remaining threads in the group. Then, using the thread directly adjacent to it, make a loop over the horizontal thread, beneath itself, over its horizontal thread once again, and lastly, through the loop you just made. Pull the knot firmly closed. Your knot will be a half hitch.

16. Continue this process with each thread till all of the ones on the left are finished.

17. Underneath a half hitch knot on the right, take the following thread. Repeat the half-hitch knotting procedure as you pull that thread across in a horizontal direction.

18. Repeat this procedure six times to create eight half-hitch knots, except the bottom one.

19. Here, you will tie the knot on the left side's bottom.

20. Grabbing the bottom knot's rightmost thread is your initial move. Then, using the thread directly adjacent to it, make a loop over the horizontal thread, beneath itself, over the horizontal thread once again, and lastly, through the loop you just made. Pull the knot firmly closed. Your knot will be a half hitch.

21. Place the thread horizontally over the other strands to tie a half-hitch knot. Using the same threads, loop them over horizontal threads and then through the loop that has been produced. It is done with the next thread. To tighten, pull

22. Next, cross the remaining threads with the thread just utilized for the horizontal thread. Three horizontal threads should be present. To tie a half hitch knot, take the threads adjacent to it and wrap them around the 3 horizontal threads. Using the same threads, loop them over horizontal threads and then through the loop that has been produced. It is done with the next thread. To tighten, pull

23. Repeat this method to the last thread, adding one thread each time.

24. Start by completing the right side in the same manner as you completed the left. The technique is the same, so if you finish the left side, you shouldn't have too much trouble. The preceding steps should be repeated.

25. If you don't understand it the first time, don't worry. Your stitching can always be undone so that you may try again.

26. Make sure the threads dangling from the right and left sides are vertical by pulling on them. The threads need to be grouped.

27. Cut a length of thread about 4 inches long and fold it in half. Place that piece of the thread now, resting on top of the bunch with the opposite edges facing up.

28. Pick one thread from the collection of threads. It should be wrapped around the threads.

29. Once there is just a little bit of a single thread remaining, keep wrapping the thread all around the collection of threads. The little length of purple thread cut previously was supposed to form a loop. For the loose thread to come out fully and the end of a single thread to get caught within the loop, make a knot, place the end of the purple thread through the loop and pull the two ends of a loose thread at the top.

30. From the knot you just made, many strands should hang loosely. To demonstrate that the threads are spaced at the same intervals, thread a tiny bead through each one. To keep each bead in place, tie an overhand knot there at the end of each one. See the prior instructions for details on how to finish this.

31. Remove any extra threads from beneath the knots.

32. You will get a lovely keychain that you may keep for yourself or give to someone else.

10. Seven Point Snowflake

Materials

- Any household clean drying fabric or glue

- Pins and Project Board

- 1 1/2 inches ring

- 1.4 yards or 2mm white cord material

Directions

1. With LHK, all cables need to be attached to the 1.5-inch ring. You may do that by folding the cord, slipping it beneath the ring, and bringing the ends down and over the top of the ring. Passing the ends across the folded region is necessary. The reverse half hitch must be made by slipping the ends through the cord, over the ring, and under the ring. This process should be followed by all other cords, after which the cords should be arranged into a group of seven with four chords. The knots should all be firmly tied off to prevent further loosening.

2. Each set of four cords should have two SK linked to it. To guarantee that the first rests on the knots on the ring, the fillers should also be tugged to tighten them firmly.

3. The two SK's four cables need to be numbered. Use cables 3 - 4 from one SK and cords One to Two from the second SK to rotate the cords. At this point, while joining the ASK in a circular ring, one must be cautious

when choosing the four cords that emanate from the two neighboring knots.

4. To finish the second row, the remaining cords should adhere to step 3.

5. The same cords should be utilized as in step 2, and the cords should alternate once more. The third row of ASK should be tied completely around the snowflake's seven points. A 1/2 inch should separate all knots from the second row from the knots inside this row.

6. Using the four cords you just finished, a picot has now been created below all of the knots from step 5. Let's resume our work now. Beneath one of your knots made in row three, an SK needs to be tied.

7. We pull the knot up to form two picot loops to ensure it sits on the knot formed in step 5 above. However, we will knot another SK near the one that was just done using the same four cords.

8. Apply glue on the fillings first, then tighten the knots. After the glue has dry, cut the ends to 1 inch, and then separate the fibers at the ends of the 7-point snowflake to create a fringe.

9. With a different pair of cables, repeat steps 6 through 8 as necessary.

10. Using cotton cable cords increases the likelihood that knots may relax with time; therefore, even though this is an optional step, that is also recommended. Putting fabric adhesive behind each knot would be best before flipping the snowflake over. Another thing to remember regarding the fabric glue that will be applied is that it has to be transparent after it dries.

Chapter 5: Advanced Projects

1. Tassels Garland

Garlands have existed since they were first used to denote beauty and purity. They provide color and festive air to whatever room they are in. This project is quite adaptable. The garland may be displayed on flat surfaces like the top of the bed's headboard or a mantle, used like a wall hanging, placed in a nursery, or even hung out of a pergola for such a special event. They seem nice in any environment.

Materials

- 3-ply cotton rope 53.8 m (5 mm diameter), recycled

- Tape measure

- A flat surface or a clipboard and washi tape

- 1 ply cotton rope 64.2 m (3 mm diameter), recycled

- Scissors

Directions

Note: Attach the long 1.8m sections of rope to a clipboard to simplify handling. After that, proceed in segments to complete the garland.

1. To begin making a tassel, fold 12 of a 0.8 m 1-ply cord in half. After threading each of the 40 cm 1-ply cords below the fold formed by the 12 cords, tie a tight knot. Another tight knot, 55 cm from the edge, is used to secure the tassel towards the 1.8 m long, three-ply cord.

2. There will now be some extra cord, but wait to cut it until you've tied the gathering knot.

3. Make a collecting knot about 3 cm long with one of the 1-ply cords that are 70 cm long.

4. Trim any extra cords and tuck them away beneath the gathering knot. Attach 8 1.3 m 3-ply cords in a reverse lark's head knot below the tassel.

5. Work the square knots in the following order:

- **Line 1:** Four square knots with cables 1 through 16.

- **Line 2:** Using cords 3–14, tie 3 square knots.

- **Line 3:** With cords 5–12, tie two square knots.

- **Line 4:** Using cords 7–10, tie a square knot.

6. Please measure the ends length from the lowest square knot and trim them to 20 cm.

7. Re-do step 1.

8. Recurring step 2.

9. Re-do step 1.

10. Repeat step 2 for the center inverted triangle, substituting five spiral knots for one square knot on line 4.

11. Once you create six tassels and five inverted triangles, alternately continue steps 1 and 2 once.

Variations: Why not manufacture colorful tassels rather than natural ones if you own colorful fibers at home?

You may choose earthy, pastel, or vibrant colors for each tassel. You may combine natural colors with one or two additional soft colors to get a more understated appearance. There are many options!

2. Macramé Curtain

Your home will have a beach house ambiance thanks to macramé curtains. You aren't even required to add any shells or trinkets, although you may if you want. Here is a fantastic macramé curtain that you can build, however.

Materials:

- Curtain rod

- Pins

- Tape

- Laundry rope (or any cord or rope you want)

- Scissors

- Lighter

Directions:

1. Four strands should be tied together, and the top knots should be pinned to keep the structure in place.

2. Take your strand on your outer right section, and pass it through the center, allowing it crosses onto the left side. Reverse after tightly pulling the ropes together.

3. Repeat crossing it over four more times for the thread you currently have in front of you. Take the outer-left strand and allow it to cross over the center. Next, please take the right strand and allow it to cross over the outer-left strand. Continue as necessary, and then split the collection of strands towards the left and the right. Continue until you get the desired number of rows.

4. It may now be used on the ropes. Gather the desired number of ropes—10 to 14 is acceptable or as many as the rod will accommodate—with enough spacing.

5. Beginning at the curtain's top, tie knots until the length you want is reached. To keep the ends from unraveling, burn or tape them. To give the ropes that enchanting seashore appearance, braid them together.

6. You may now utilize your new curtain after that.

3. Table Runner

Due to its loose weave, the macramé table runner won't perform the conventional function of keeping your tablecloth clean. It will, however, offer visual appeal to your table's cape. It offers a striking contrast and looks great on the rustic wooden desk or the upper edge of a dark-cleaned linen tablecloth.

Materials

- 150.80 m braided cotton rope (5 mm diameter), natural

- Scissors

- A dowel with a minimum diameter of 3 cm, since the length of fringes, will be determined by this

- Tape measure

- Large eye knitting needle

Directions

Tip: Use your fingers to ensure the knots are as tight and close together as you can for a horizontal double half-hitch knot. It prevents the design from being wacky. Try to apply the same pressure to each square knot to create the most uniform-looking design. This project may be completed in either a vertical or flat location. You must begin standing up and end up seated on the floor if you wish to create it vertically. Using washi or masking tape to secure your work towards the table and wall you are creating is usually simpler. Utilize the extra rope from this project to make other things!

1. Start using a lark's head knot to attach your 20-long cords to the dowel.

2. Use the horizontal double half hitch knot to attach the 40 working cords to 1 of the 40 cm long cables.

- **Line 1:** Make a berry knot using cords 19–22.

3. Create a pyramid form by continuing the process, removing 2 wires from the left side and connecting 2 cords to the right.

- **Line 2:** Use cords 17–24 to tie two square knots.

- **Line 3:** Employer Using cords 15–26, tie three square knots.

- **Line 4:** Use cords 13 to 28 to tie four square knots.

- **Line 5:** Use cords 11 to 30 to tie 5 square knots.

- **Line 6:** Using cords 9-32, tie six square knots.

- **Line 7:** Tie seven square knots with cables 7 to 34.

- **Line 8:** Utilizing cords 5-36, tie 8 square knots.

- **Line 9:** Use cords 3-38 to tie nine square knots.

- **Line 10:** Use cords 1 through 40 to tie 10 square knots.

- **Line 11:** Duplicate line 10 and tie 10 square knots with cords 1–40.

4. Continue step 4 in reverse, beginning from line 11 through line 1, leaving a 10 cm space between each repetition. Rather than a berry knot, tie one square knot in line 1 this time.

5. Using cords 9–12, tie a square knot 10 cm up from the bottom of the final square knot. Use cords 7–14 to tie two more square knots right behind the first. Making a square knot using cords 9–12 completes this diamond design. Use cords 29-32 (One square knot) for the first line, 27-34 (2 square knots) for the second line, and 29-32 (One square knot) once again for the third and final line. Repeat this step on the right side of the table runner.

6. The table runner's large diamond-shaped center, which you will now make, is a square knot.

7. Follow the directions below to make your design, allowing a 10 cm gap:

- **Line 1:** Utilizing cords 19–22, tie one square knot.

- **Line 2:** Use cords 17–24 to tie two square knots.

- **Line 3:** Employer Using cords 15–26, tie three square knots.

- **Line 4:** Utilizing cords 13–28, tie four square knots.

- **Line 5:** Using cords 11–30, tie five square knots.

- **Line 6:** Work Using cords 9–32, tie six square knots.

- **Line 7:** Work, using cords 7–34, and tie seven square knots.

- **Line 8:** Utilizing cords 5-36, tie 8 square knots.

- **Line 9:** Activity working with cables 3-38, ties 9 square knots.

- **Line 10:** Tie 10 square knots.

- **Line 11:** Work Using cables 3-38, tie 9 square knots.

- **Line 12:** Using cords 5-36, tie 8 square knots.

- **Line 13:** Activity Using cords 7–34, tie seven square knots.

- **Line 14:** Use cords 9 to 32 to tie six square knots.

- **Line 15:** Work Using cords 11–30, tie five square knots.

- **Line 16:** Work Using cords 13–28, tie four square knots.

- **Line 17:** Work Using cords 15–26, tie three square knots.

- **Line 18:** Using cords 17–24, tie two square knots.

- **Line 19:** Work, Making a square knot with cords 19–22

8. Re-do step 6.

9. Repeat steps 3 and 4 to create 11 additional lines, allowing an additional 10 cm from the bottom square knot previously tied in step 8. This time, make a regular square knot rather than beginning the top of the triangle with a berry knot.

10. Perform steps 4 & 3 in the opposite sequence, leaving a 10 cm gap. Starting with line 11 and continuing until the line

11. This time, as instructed in step 3, you will complete the inverted triangle by tying a berry knot.

12. From chord 1, leave an 11.5 cm space. Use the horizontal double half hitch knot to attach the 40 working cables to the second 40 cm long cord.

13. Cut the tops of the hoops to form the fringe, untie a double half-hitch knot, and take out the dowel.

14. Trim this bottom fringe to a length of about 10 cm, matching the top. After tying the ends of a horizontal half-hitch knot behind a table runner using a big eye-knitting needle, you're done.

4. Textured Wall Hanging

People especially like stacking and melodically mixing various knots. The medium-sized wall hanging is very beautifully contoured. However, sometimes you want a raw, natural, and more "imperfectly flawless" aesthetic. Using braided rope keeps your knots exceedingly tidy. These midsize wall hangings use a 3-ply recycled cotton rope is precisely what it provides.

Materials

- 13.2 m of 1-ply cotton rope, recycled, having a 3 mm diameter

- 2 hooks

- Scissors

- 97.4 m of 3-ply cotton rope, recycled, having a 5 mm diameter

- 30 cm wooden dowel

- Tape measure

Directions

Tip: You may roll the ends of the rope into a little ball to make them shorter if you find working with long rope sections difficult since they tend to become tangled easily. Consider a little ball of yarn!

1. Start using a lark's head knot to secure 3 x 3.7 m long cords on the dowel's left end and 3 additional cords on the dowel's right end.

2. Use the diamond pattern procedures to create 3 diamonds per each side.

3. Create the right diagonal double half hitch knot with cords 5 and 6 using cord 4 as your anchor cord. Use cord 9 as the anchor & cords 8 and 7 as your working cords to tie a left diagonal double half hitch knot. Connect cords six and seven with a knot. Cut all of these cables down to 30 cm.

4. Install two 2 x 3 m long, one-ply cables six centimeters from the left end of the dowel, then carry out the same procedure with the remaining 2 x 3 m long cords, allowing six centimeters now at the right end of the dowel.

5. Work spiral knots measuring 23 cm on both sides. Utilize the 0.6 m length 1 ply rope to tie them together. Make a gathering knot 3 cm long, ensuring the spirals precisely frame the diamonds you created in step 2.

Save the trimmings for later use and cut the tail to 30 cm below the gathering knot.

6. Prepare to work on the last diamonds of this wall hanging. Install 4 cords, each 3.7 meters long, on the left and right sides of a spiral knot. Reposition these lark's head knots with your hands so that there is still 1 cm of dowel on both sides. On each side, work 4 diamonds. Next time, you will enclose each diamond in a square knot. After completing the top half of every diamond, tie a square knot with cords 2 and 7 as the working cords.

7. Use cords 5-8 and 12-09 to tie them together using a right diagonal double half hitch knot and a left double half hitch knot, respectively. Use a double half-hitch knot to join the two leading cords. Create another diamond with the following 4 strands per each side using 2 leading cords.

8. This step is not required. You may leave this last diamond's inside unfilled. Those x 1-ply trimmings you put aside in step 4 will be used with 4 of them if you decide to remain with the original design. To make a tassel, cut it in half and tie a rya knot. It should be cut to 12 cm. You may comb the tassel if you want. Ours is uncombed to give it a rough feel. Make sure that all the rope you have used is the same length.

9. It's time to add the side tassels to complete the wall hanging. You can notice that the diamonds you just made have formed four complete loops from one to the below if you glance at the outside of them. Lark's head knots attach individual tassels one at a time to these hoops. Given that they are a little smaller than the rest, the top left and right hoops only need the addition of three tassels. Everyone else will get 4. Each tassel should be attached to the string that forms the loop's outermost segment. Add all of the tassels at once. All that is left to do is clip any cable that is bigger than the rest.

10. To create a triangle on the dowel and hang your new item on the wall with pride, add the final 0.6 m of cord.

5. Dream Catcher

Since childhood, dream catchers have attracted me. It would be best if you were enthralled by the concept of a woven web that would trap negative dreams while allowing tranquil ones to slip through. It would be best if you made a little homage by making your macramé dream catcher. The chance to work using macramé feathers is fantastic as well.

Materials:

- 1 ply recycled cotton 31.35 m having 5 mm diameter

- Scissors

- Face mask

- 25 cm hoop, wooden

- Tape measure

- Slicker brush

Directions:

Note: To create the feathers simpler to produce, we will utilize sections that are 20 cm long. If you have already created macramé feathers, you may cut the feather parts a little shorter. Instead, clip 140 pieces of string at a length of 15 cm.

1. One 60 cm long cotton cord should be folded in half before being knotted with a reverse lark's head knot to the wooden hoop.

2. To install into the feather stem you just made, set aside 28 pieces of 20 cm long rope. Half-fold 1 piece. Put it beneath the focal point. The second cotton rope is folded in half and placed over the centerpiece. Pull the ends after bringing them through the loops on both sides. Repeat this procedure when you have tied 14 knots and are out of rope. Repeat steps 1 & 2 four more times to get five feathers. Brush your feathers while wearing your face mask. Use your fingers to separate each feather from the others as you brush each separately.

3. Till the cotton is smooth, brush it away. Do the same with the other feathers. If you need more room to thoroughly brush each one, don't forget to shift them about.

4. It's time to cut them. They measure 7 centimeters in length. The feathers should be repositioned 5 cm apart. Use a lark's head knot to attach your 35 cm long one-ply cotton rope to the top of a wooden hoop. To hang the dream catcher, make a knot now at the end.

Changes: If you'd like a more colorful dream catcher, you may use various colored ropes or dye your cotton with natural dyes.

6. Square Cushion Cover

If you're up for a little challenge, the cushion cover art is extra detailed than the last one. This style focuses on texture with fringes to give your room a little movement plus a romantic feel.

Materials

- A cushion cover of 40 x 40 cm

- Masking tape or washi tape

- Warp thread

- Scissors

- A dowel with a minimum diameter of 3 cm, like the length of fringes, will be determined by this

- 107.7 m braided cotton rope natural having a 5 mm diameter

- Large eye knitting needle

- Tape measure

Directions

Tip: For cushions like this one, you will often find it simpler to work inside a vertical posture. Please ensure the horizontal double half hitch knots are as tight as possible while working on them. Adjust the lark's head knots on your dowel using fingers if the line of knots begins to sag, but only up to the size of the cushion cover, which is 40 cm. A 0.55 cm filler cord's end may be attached to the wall using washi tape in step four. Working on the initial horizontal double half hitch knot will be simpler. On each side, leaving about 9 cm extra filler cord. If you don't want a fringed cushion, you may use the big eye knitting needle to thread the fringe pieces into the back of horizontal double half-hitch knots. The extra rope may then be trimmed and sewn to a cushion cover.

1. Apply lark's head knots to the 26 4 m long ropes to secure them to the dowel. Work one row of horizontal double half hitch knots - left to right on one of the 1.30

m long ropes, using it as the filler cord. Place the remaining filler on top of your work after tying the last knot, then tie the second row of horizontal double half-hitches from right to left.

2. Square knots should be worked in 3 rows, with a 1 cm space between each row. These three rows should be 6.5 to 7 cm apart. If yours differs from this, we advise you to redo or change your knots, so they are the same length as the cushion cover.

3. From left to right, tie a series of horizontal double half hitch knots with the 0.55 m long rope like the filler cord.

4. Divide the leftover ropes into 4 sets of 14- 12- 14- 14 ropes each, and then use diagonal double half hitch knots to form 4 diamond shapes. Work the left diagonal double half hitch knot starting with cable number 7, ending at cord number 1, and starting with chord number 7. Using cord 8, tie the right diagonal double half hitch knot until cord number 14 is reached. As you can see, your new cord number 1 will be your original cord number 7, and the new cord number 14 will be your original cord number 8. Create one loose square knot using ropes 2 and 13 using the materials. If you want the filler cords to remain as flat as possible, you may adjust them with your fingertips. To create the

bottom of the diamond, tie a double half-hitch knot using the right and left diagonals. Make a dual knot using cords seven and eight to complete it.

5. Repeat this process, making sure to use 12 ropes for each of the two diamonds inside the middle and 14 ropes for the final diamond on the right. Between diamonds 1 and 2, tie a square knot with the two ropes furthest to the right and left, respectively. On the final two gaps, repeat this.

6. Tie two double half hitch knots on cords numbers 20 and 21 and 32 and 33 to change the height of the two middle diamonds relative to the larger ones on the sides.

7. Repetition of steps five to seven.

8. Repeat steps 4, 3, and 2.

9. Lean flat on a table while carefully removing your artwork from the dowel.

10. To make the fringe for your cushion, unfold the lark's head knots you formed in step 1 and cut every rope where the knot is in the middle. Cut the fringes at about the same length from the opposite end.

11. Turn your work over and cut the extra rope before threading the tails of horizontal double half-hitch knots with the big eye knitting needle.

12. Place the 40 x 40 cm cushion cover of your choice on top of your macramé creation, and then stitch the cushion cover's edges to the macramé using the big eye knitting needle and warp thread. The cushion is finished.

7. Macramé Mirror

Mirrors are a terrific method to reflect light throughout a space, particularly if you place them next to a lamp or opposite windows. Mirrors are popular because they make tiny rooms seem larger. Decorate your foyer, main bedroom, or nursery with this lovely textured macramé mirror to make a statement.

Materials

- 23 cm mirror, round

- Tape measure

- Hot glue and glue gun

- Hoop with a 20 cm diameter. Any kind of material is acceptable. With this project, We went with copper

- 60.25 m of 1-ply cotton rope with having 3 mm diameter, recycled

- Scissors

- Macramé slicker brush

Directions

Tip: Choose EVA hot glue sticks if you share our concern about the effects of hot glue on the environment. Although they still have a plastic foundation, which is terrible, they are expected to degrade more quickly, unlike other synthetic materials.

1. Install the first six cords, each 75 cm long, to the hoop using a lark's head knot.

2. Tend a row of three square knots using cords 1-4, 5-8, and 9-12. With cords 3-6 and 7-10, tie two square knots in a second row. The design will begin to resemble an upside-down triangle. Finally, using cords 5-8, tie a square knot for the third row.

3. You can frame this inverted triangle by tying 2 diagonal double half-hitch knots on each side.

4. The fringe should be 2.5 cm long. Use some tape to help you cut this as straight as you can.

5. Prepare your face mask! The fringe has to be brushed now. Take your brush and put on your face mask. Brush your fringe until every thread has come undone. The end of the fringe will develop some cotton fluff when you brush the cotton. Once you're done, cut it to give it a neater appearance.

6. You will now create a more compact inverted triangle. To do this, tie a lark's head knot adjacent to the inverted triangle you created and install four pieces of cord measuring 40 cm each into your hoops.

7. Tie one row of square knots with cords 1-4 and 5-8. Using cords 3-6, tie the second row of one square knot. Make 2 diagonal double half-hitch knots across each side to form a frame for your little, inverted triangle. Continue with steps five and six until the hoop is full. Fold the nearby inverted triangle and set it back down after you're done if it is in the way.

8. Make a quite tight double knot only at the end of a 30 cm long rope after folding it in half. Working a lark's head knot, attach this cord to the hoop. Between the two square knots from one of the little triangles, we will

tie this piece in place. Apply a little amount of adhesive with a glue gun to the back of a macramé piece—the inner edge of a rim is a good location—and attach it firmly to your mirror for 10 to 15 seconds to make sure it sticks.

8. Jute Plant Hanger

One of the people's favorite fibers is jute. Jute, originally from India and made from the plant Corchorus olitorius or Corchorus capsularis, give your creations a wonderful texture that makes them seem quite cozy and natural. Jute is a good material to use if you want a plant hanger that you can put on a porch since it doesn't absorb water as effectively as cotton.

Materials

- 2 m jute rope having 2 mm diameter
- Tape measure
- Hook
- 24 m jute rope with having 6 mm diameter
- 5 cm wooden ring
- Scissors

Directions

Tip: A jute hanger should not be left all the time outdoors since water will eventually seep through the fiber and destroy your lovely product. This natural fiber may not be the softest material, therefore, exercise caution while dealing with it because of its nature. Once you tighten the knots, go slowly.

1. In a hook, hang the wooden ring. Six pieces of jute string should be threaded through the wooden ring. The simplest method to achieve this is to thread the six pieces of rope through the ring collectively rather than one at a time. Each side of a ring should have a string about the same length.

2. Make a collecting knot about 3 cm long out of one piece of 2 mm broad jute.

3. The 12 cords should be divided into three groups of 4. Make five square knots with the first set of four ropes. With the remaining 2 groups, repeat this.

4. To deal with the inner cords, which are now located on the outside, take your outermost cords and slide them between the inner cords, leaving a space of 10 cm. By doing this, you may avoid using the same cables throughout your project or going out of the cord until it is complete.

5. Make two square knots, then ten spiral knots, then two more square knots to complete the knot. In the three groups, repeat this.

6. Pick the Two right-hand cords of whatever group plus the two left-hand cords of a group towards the right, leaving a 20 cm space between them. Make two square knots using these 4 ropes. Repeat this procedure twice, working to your right, to connect all the cables.

7. Repeat step 6 while leaving about 8 cm of space. This time, tie one square knot alone. Make a collecting knot about 3 cm long with the additional piece of thin jute. Your preferred length for the plant hanger's tail should be used. This one will be cut at 25 cm.

9. Diamonds and Tassels Wall Hanging

People like making tassels. They give any work more life, texture, and character. This beautiful wall-hanging design mixes a variety of intriguing knots to give it several dimensionalities.

Materials

- 30 cm wooden dowel

- Tape measure

- 59.4 m braided cotton with having 5 mm diameter

- 2 hooks

- Scissors

Directions

Tip: Feeling artistic? We will use braided cotton for tassels, but you may also try 1 ply cotton rope or braided cotton in other colors. Tassels made of one-ply cotton rope may be combed to make them seem exquisitely tidy. For this, it would be best to utilize the groom's slicker brush containing fine stainless steel pins. Make sure the pins don't have plastic tips, however. When combing your tassels, please wear a face mask since there will be plenty of cotton lint floating about.

1. Mount a wooden dowel while tying 16 larks' head knots with the cotton cords.

2. Work four rows of square knots alternately, attempting to apply the same pressure to each knot.

3. Use cords 1 through 8 to create a macramé diamond design (left to right). Grab cords two and seven and tie a square knot with them after you have finished the top of the diamond. You've only tied square knots with four cords thus far. This time, you'll create chords 2 and 7, while cords 3, 4, 5 and 6 will serve as filler cables. Finish the diamond's bottom now. To make a row of four macramé diamonds repeat step 3 once more.

4. Working cords 6, 7, and 8 are tied to the anchor using the right diagonal double half hitch knot using cord 5 as the anchor. Reverse step 5 now. Working cords 11, 10, and 9 are tied to the anchor using the left diagonal

double half hitch knot using cord 12 as the anchor. Double-half hooks the two anchor cables together.

5. Use cables 13 to 20 & 21 to 28 to do step 5 again.

6. Using cables 9 to 16 & 17 to 24, repeat step 5.

7. Apply steps 5 to cables 13 through 20.

8. The tassels need to be added now. Make one rya knot in closed and open diamonds using six cords that are each 30 cm long, as shown in the illustration. Move up from the lowest starting point. After creating the six tassels, cut them to a length of 10 cm to make them equal.

9. Attach one 0.6 cm piece to the dowel using the piece. Your work is prepared to be hung.

10. Raffia Leaf

Influenced by cotton macramé leaves, this leaf. You may hang it on a wall, doorknob, or ornamental ladder to add a unique and eye-catching piece of décor to your room.

Materials

- 300 gr having natural raffia, 6 bundles of 50 gr

- Scissors

- 130 cm out of 6 mm jute rope

- Tape measure

Directions

Tip: Once you're done, you may use the steamer to create the raffia more flexibly if you want to somewhat tame the leaf. This sculpture may be built vertically on the wall or horizontally on a flat surface. Since this form of crafting is simpler on a horizontal surface, we shall do it there. You should cut a large amount of raffia. Therefore, it is advised that you do it on a simple surface to sweep and avoid carpeting or rugs.

1. The jute cord is folded in half. Make a loop knot, leaving about 10 cm of space at the top. The spine of the leaf will be made of this cord.

2. Depending on how thick each raffia fiber is, split approximately 18 - 20 pieces into two groups of 9 or 10.

3. The raffia should now be fastened toward the centerpiece. Given that individual pieces of raffia might vary in length take the first bundle and fold it into half or as near as you can. Put it beneath the focal point. Over the centerpiece, position the second raffia bundle, which has been folded in half. Through the loops on both sides, pass the ends. The right will pass through the right loop, while the left ends will do the same. Next, pull. You may do this after completing the step and trimming the raffia to the desired length. The raffia leaf is cut at 20 cm across both sides for the project.

4. The third step is 32 times. The new leaf is prepared to hang after you tie one loop knot at the bottom.

Variations: Try experimenting with other fibers, like banana fiber, to create movement in the sculpture.

11.   Market Bag

For the past five years, avoiding plastic has been our primary goal. Reusable tote bags are quite popular among those who go shopping. This market bag serves as a daily all-purpose tote bag and is ideal for picking up food at your neighborhood farmer's market.

Materials

- 54.8 m natural braided cotton rope with having 5 mm diameter

- Scissors

- A flat surface or a clipboard and washi tape

- Tape measure

Directions

Tip: For this kind of activity, particularly Step 3, using a clipboard will be simpler. If you don't own a clipboard, you may use masking tape to fix the project's sides to a wall.

1. Make the indicated knot with the two pieces of 1 m cotton cord for handles. To make this, fold each cord into half and then slip the folded ends under to form a loop. Afterward, pass them through the loop. Ensure that both end wires are together as you pull firmly. Check that the knot is tied on the second rope using the same procedure, being sure to make it at the exact height of the initial handle.

2. You can create the bag's body by using 12 lark head knots on each side to secure the cords toward the handles.

3. To assemble your bag, tie two pieces together using this identical knot in rows of alternating square knots. Each group begins by tying the square knots' first row.

4. Remember to leave the initial and final 2 cords free while you complete a final row of alternating square knots. Then, tie a third row of square knots utilizing the cords.

5. On the fourth row, you must begin joining the two parts together. The lark's head knots should be facing on both sides as you stack them one above the other. Like you've been doing, leave a 1 cm space and tie a square knot

with the two cords from the leftmost group of both groups. Continue on the right side. Complete the fourth row of the square knots on the bag's front and rear. Try to align the square knots on both sides at an equal height.

6. Up until you've completed 13 rows, alternately tie square knots 1 cm apart.

7. Make three rows of alternating square knots spaced 2 cm apart to give the design a little "Je ne sais quois."

8. Using the leftmost string on the front and your leftmost cord from the rear of the bag, make a knot exactly as you did for the handles to create the bottom of the bag. On the right side of the bag, repeat this. Tie square knots to connect the bag's front and back, forming the center. The bottom should be solidly constructed. Please take the next two left cords from the bag's rear and, starting from the left, use them as the leading ropes for the square knot. The two left cables from the bag's front are the fillings. Put a knot in a square. With the remaining knots, repeat this method.

9. The tassels should be trimmed to the desired height or cut off at 14 cm.

Variations: Add pompoms, a long tassel, or anything else amusing to one of the handles for a summertime appearance. Be imaginative!

Chapter 6: Business with Macramé

How to Effectively Sell Macramé Products on Etsy?

Here, we'll go through the major components of selling successfully on Etsy, from developing a crucial rapport with consumers to ensuring prospective buyers can locate your products. As you follow this section, consider maintaining your Etsy listings and marketing as one component of a successful, skilled worker company. You must deliver the goods to your clients as soon as possible and profitably when the orders start flowing in. Etsy is a huge platform for showcasing and selling your artistic creations. Etsy provides a comprehensive platform for selling goods and attracts a sizable purchasing crowd of viewers looking for remarkable products. The greatest way to succeed on Etsy is to make your products stand out from the competition, which involves regular work. Therefore, it's important to determine whether selling via Etsy is the correct choice for you before diving into the how-to of doing so.

Here are three inquiries you need to make of yourself:

1. Do my items meet Etsy's highest profit price point?

Several successful Etsy stores with regular merchandise priced at or over $50. Etsy editors know that cheaper prices attract a larger proportion of customers. Therefore, they successfully look for merchants with respect ratings under $50 to put in their customary Editor's Picks sections.

2. Do we possess the necessary particular skills to influence Etsy?

At the very least, having a solid working knowledge of getting and transmitting messages, taking and editing product photos, and navigating drop-down menus on websites is important. Etsy is incredibly intuitive and amazingly quick to use when you receive the hang of one's dashboard. On the off chance that you are new to electronic selling, there is a need to learn and modify.

3. Are we willing to set aside my desire to complete most of the Etsy criteria for the course of action, moving on, and packing and shipping?

Despite low support concerns, producing works, posting and promoting them on Etsy, attending to customer inquiries, and finally pressing and expressing things require effort. It takes more than just placing items on a website and hoping for the best to sell stuff on Etsy.

Beautiful Pictures

All the consistent work you put into building up your products and brand can be undone in a matter of seconds by a terrible photograph or crippling product depiction. The next step is to concentrate on presenting your products in the best possible light now that you know how to relate with the customers. The main method a prospective buyer may see works and assess the concept of your items is via photographs. Amazing photos are, therefore, crucial to understanding how to sell on Etsy and are the most remarkable aspect of product presentation. Five photos can be used with each posting on Etsy. You may need them to showcase every aspect of your artistic endeavors. Nevertheless, your photographs must be stunning if you want to succeed with your Etsy sales.

Have Prompt and Approachable Buyer Communications

Keep monitoring the Etsy message box because customers will send you various demands and offers. It is standard practice to reply to these communications within one business day. This tactfulness conveys the idea of a well-defined approach and, in addition, shows the client how much you appreciate their time and possible business.

Create a Relationship with Your Customers

Step-by-step advice on how to build a brand and sell on Etsy. No matter how unique a product is, it's almost certain that people on Etsy are offering a similar item. Considering everything, how might you stand out from the competition and persuade clients to choose your items over other vendors? The appropriate response is to stamp.

Create enticing and precise item descriptions

Your chance to draw prospective clients and vocally entice them to purchase is via the representation of your goods. Take a conversational approach while creating your representations. You must provide important product information, but do it charmingly and alluringly.

Chapter 7: Tips and Tricks

A place where you may let your thoughts roam and refresh, macramé nourishes the soul. That goal is defeated if you struggle with fraying, tangled cords or fringe that won't behave the way you want it to. To help you, we've compiled a list of our best macramé hints and suggestions. With these tips at your disposal, you'll macramé like a pro and stay out of trouble while enjoying the rhythm of knotting.

1. It might be challenging to tie a straight row with double half-hitch knots, particularly if you're new to macramé.

To make this procedure easier, position a dowel rod where you want to start making the row with double half-hitch knots.

2. Still having trouble getting the fringe clipped straight?

Cut the fringe below the knot after bundling it together with a working cord.

The fringe must be pretty straight when you untie the knot. It may always be reduced till it meets your standards.

3. Finding the proper cord length might be challenging, particularly if you're coming up with your design rather than using a pre-existing template.

Fortunately, there is a workaround: how many knots you use will decide how much rope you need.

As a general guideline, cords should be measured at least four times longer than are needed for your project.

Double the length if you secure these cords using lark's head knots.

3.5 times the overall project length is sufficient for straightforward projects with straightforward knots, plenty of fringes, and open space in the design.

The project duration would need to be increased by 4.5 for complex projects.

4. You have extensive rope lengths available while working on a big project.

Keeping things organized while working is a challenge since they often get intertwined.

So why not make balls out of these long lines and secure them with rubber bands? Thus, the cables are kept tidy.

Pull a little bit off the balls; you need an extra string to work with as the project develops.

5. Fringes on finished items often behave like beach hair: they fly about and make a mess.

Brush and steam the fringe before applying hair spray or fabric stiffener to stop this from occurring.

You now have a flawless fringe that will always remain in place.

6. It doesn't have to take long to measure the cord. We offer a workaround if your project calls for several cables of the same length.

Two dowel sticks, each half the length of the cable you require, should be taped to your work area.

Now, wrap the cord once around each dowel according to the length you need. At once, cut through each loop.

Yes! There, at the ideal length, are all the cables you need.

7. Due to its constant movement, cutting a fringe on your most recent work might discomfort your neck.

After holding the fringe in position with tape, cut along the tape.

You now have a flawless fringe that stayed put when you trimmed it.

8. Everyone makes errors, and sometimes doing so requires unraveling a whole area of work. Fortunately, it's not always necessary to go on a mission.

Pull on the anchor rope to undo a row tied of double half hitch knots. The whole row should be simple to loosen up.

9. When you're engaged in a project, the cord often unfolds.

When dealing with the 3-ply cord, tie the cord ends in a knot or secure them in tape to prevent this from occurring.

10. Have trouble establishing consistent distances between the knot patterns?

Apply a spacer! In this case, you might cut one piece of cardboard towards the required size or use a dowel or ruler.

You may now design your macramé masterpiece with precisely spaced designs.

Conclusion

With a little effort, anyone can learn how to make macramé, a beautiful knotting craft. It's a terrific method to make stunning and useful works of art to add vintage style to your home décor. Depending on the ability level, macramé is a highly intriguing type of art that is simple to master but can be utilized in various ways. Simple bracelets and intricate wall hangings may be made by combining knots, loops, and braiding. You can create so many different things with just one craft. It's incredible. The origins of macramé may be found in ancient Egypt. By mixing loops, knots, and braiding, artisans learned how to make various items, from simple bracelets to intricate wall hangings, including cloth garlands for adults and kids. The 18th century saw the invention of the word "macramé." To master macramé, one must practice a lot and have patience.

Nevertheless, learning is worthwhile since it offers so many advantages. Compared to other art types, macramé is less costly since all the materials are readily available at practically any sewing shop, such as thread, fabric, and anchors. Even if you wish to spend more money on ornamental items, the basic five components can be utilized for many macramé projects. It's also quite simple to learn macramé. Since most of your time is spent generating your pattern, it does not take much practice to become proficient at producing objects with it.

You'll undoubtedly appreciate the advantages after you've mastered the skill of macramé. The world over, crafts and arts have traditionally been well-liked pastimes that individuals of various ages and skill levels may enjoy. You can create so many different things with just one craft. It's incredible. Because it is so straightforward and flexible in its applications, this art form was already practiced for millennia. This craft is also good for the environment. While handcrafted macramé is the most common style, this alternative enables you to design without harming the environment and yourself. Many individuals may love macramé since it doesn't need specific skills to produce spectacular things. If you want more visually beautiful and detailed outcomes, macramé will require some effort to master.

Made in United States
Troutdale, OR
12/09/2023

15575199R00064